An Island Alphabet

Erica Rutherford

RAGWEED
THE ISLAND PUBLISHER

For Nadine Turner,
who fell in love with Prince Edward Island.

Ragweed Press acknowledges the generous support of the Canada Council and
the Canada/PEI Cooperation Agreement on Cultural Development.

Printed and bound in Hong Kong by:
Wing King Tong

Published by:
Ragweed Press
P.O. Box 2023
Charlottetown, P.E.I.
Canada C1A 7N7

Distributed in Canada by:
General Distribution Services

CANADIAN CATALOGUING IN PUBLICATION DATA

Rutherford, Erica.

An Island alphabet

ISBN 0-921556-44-6

1. Prince Edward Island — Pictorial works —
Juvenile literature.   2. Alphabet — Juvenile
literature.   I. Title.

FC2611.2.R87 1994   j971.7   C94-950040-2
F1047.4.R87 1994

Abegweit **Aa**

Bb

Belfast church

Ceilidh

Cc

Dd

Dalvay dunes

East Point

Ff

Fishing

Gg

Gold Cup and Saucer

Harbour

Hh

Ii

Ice breaker

Japanese wedding

Jj

Kk

King's
Playhouse

Ll
Mm

Lucy Maud
Montgomery

Nn

National Park

Orwell Corner

Pp

Phantom
Ship

Qq

Queen Street

Rustic road

Rr

Ss

Stormstayed

Tubers

Tt

Uu

Underwater

Vv

Village Acadien

Ww
Wildflowers

Xx
Xanthia lutea

Yacht club

Yy

Zz

Zoom lens

Notes

Aa Abegweit *(aa´-beh-gwit)* Abegweit is one of the names that the Mi'kmaq (Micmac) people gave to Prince Edward Island. It means "cradled on the waves." The children in this picture are playing a game on the shore at Lennox Island, where some Mi'kmaq people from the Lennox Island Band live.

Bb Belfast church This church at Belfast was built in 1824 by settlers from Scotland. The settlers were brought to the Island by Lord Selkirk on ships called the *Polly*, the *Dykes* and the *Oughton*. You can see the graves of some of the settlers in the graveyard.

Cc Ceilidh *(kay´-lee)* A ceilidh is a Scottish clan gathering. A clan is a group of families that are related to each other. At a ceilidh people dance, play the fiddle and the bagpipes, tell stories, and eat and drink Scottish food. Sometimes there are even highland games, like in this picture.

Dd Dalvay dunes The girl in the purple swimsuit is standing in the sand dunes of Dalvay Beach. Dalvay has some of the best white sand dunes on Prince Edward Island. A short walk from the dunes is the well-known Island hotel, Dalvay-by-the-Sea.

Ee East Point East Point is the most easterly point of land on Prince Edward Island. The lighthouse at East Point was built in 1867. It was built where three tides meet: one from the Atlantic Ocean, one from the Gulf of St. Lawrence, and one from the Northumberland Strait. In the fall, East Point is the last stop for migrating birds leaving the Island.

Ff Fishing Many people on the Island make their living from fishing. In this picture you can see some fishing boats and lobster traps. Lobsters are one of the main kinds of seafood caught on the Island.

Gg Gold Cup and Saucer The Gold Cup and Saucer horse race takes place in Charlottetown during "Old Home Week." This is a week in August when many Islanders who now live in other places come home to visit relatives and friends. The Gold Cup and Saucer is one of the biggest races in the Maritimes.

Hh Harbour Here is a harbour like many of the harbours you can see on the Island. Horses are helping to harvest Irish Moss, while herons look for food in the shallow water.

Ii Ice breaker Ferries that cut through ice are called ice breakers. You can see them in winter, when the Northumberland Strait between Prince Edward Island and Nova Scotia freezes over.

Jj Japanese wedding Many visitors from Japan come to the Island to see the home of writer Lucy Maud Montgomery and her fictional heroine Anne of Green Gables. Some Japanese visitors marry in Park Corner, where Lucy Maud Montgomery was married.

Kk King's Playhouse In the summertime, you can go to the King's Playhouse in Georgetown and watch plays put on by a local theatre group. The building was designed in 1898 by an Island architect named William Critchlow Harris. In 1983, the King's Playhouse caught fire and had to be rebuilt.

Ll Mm Lucy Maud Montgomery Lucy Maud Montgomery is the Island's most famous author. Her best-known book is *Anne of Green Gables*. That book, like much of her writing, shows her love for the landscape and people of Prince Edward Island.

Nn National Park The National Park was created to protect popular places such as Green Gables and Cavendish beach and other fragile areas along the shore. In the National Park, the delicate plant and animal life in the sand dunes, beaches and salt marshes is carefully watched and preserved.

Oo Orwell Corner   If you go to Orwell Corner, you can step back in time and see what it was like to live in an Island farm village in 1864. Some of the buildings you can see there are a farmhouse and post office, a general store and dressmaker's shop, a church, a school, a community hall, a blacksmith's shop, a shingle mill and animal barns.

Pp Phantom Ship   For many years, people who watch the Island shoreline have seen something they call the Phantom Ship. What they see is a burning ship with three masts that disappears as soon as anyone comes near it. According to the legend, the best time to see the ghostly ship is in the fall during a northeast wind.

Qq Queen Street   Queen Street is the main street in Charlottetown. It has downtown shops, restaurants and a theatre. In the summer, tourists like to stroll along Queen Street.

Rr Rustic road   The Island has some beautiful, unpaved roads through quiet places. These are known as rustic roads. Many kinds of flowers, plants, trees and small animals can be found along them.

Ss Stormstayed   When winter storms bury roads and cars and houses, Islanders stay at home, light their wood fires and say that they are "stormstayed." Being stormstayed is a familiar part of life on the Island in winter.

Tt Tubers   Tubers are plants with thick stems that grow underground. The potato is a tuber. In this picture you can see farmers harvesting potatoes, the most important crop on Prince Edward Island. Some Island potatoes are grown to be eaten at the table, some are made into French fries and potato chips and some, called seed potatoes, are used to grow even more potatoes.

Uu Underwater   With the help of a mask and snorkel, the girl in this painting can see some of the rich underwater life in the Atlantic Ocean. The ocean is very important to many Islanders, both for work (such as fishing and gathering Irish Moss) and for play (such as swimming and sailing).

Vv Village Acadien   The Village Acadien is at Mont-Carmel in Prince County. When you walk along the street there, you can get an idea of what it was like to live in an Acadian village many years ago. The Acadians are descendants of the first French settlers who came to the Island in the 1700s. The large stone church in this painting is called Eglise Notre-Dame du Mont-Carmel. It was built by the Acadians in 1898.

Ww Xx Wildflowers, Xanthia lutea *(zan´-thee-ah loo´-tee-ah)*
Here are some of the wildflowers that can be found on Prince Edward Island. See if you can identify these ones: wild roses, Lady-slippers (the provincial flower), wild strawberry plants, lupins, blue violets and Black-eyed Susans. Note the colourful moth beside the flowers. Its scientific name is *Xanthia lutea* and it can be seen on the Island in the fall.

Yy Yacht club   Here is the Summerside yacht club. Summerside is one of only two cities on the Island. The other city is the capital, Charlottetown. Both Summerside and Charlottetown have yacht clubs downtown, on the waterfront.

Zz Zoom lens   *An Island Alphabet* ends with a look through a zoom lens. Now turn to the first picture in the book (Abegweit). What stays the same and what changes when you look through this zoom lens?